A HOW TO HIRE: WHAT TO DO TO HIRE EMPLOYEES IN FLORIDA

The Right way

Arturo C. Guevara

A HOW TO HIRE: WHAT TO DO TO HIRE EMPLOYEES IN FLORIDA
The Right Way

1825 Ponce de Leon Blvd • # 616
Coral Gables, FL 33134
Phone (786)720-2371 • Email: amexamex@gmail.com

First Edition, 2019

ISBN xxxxxxx

"Always do the things in the right way but if you make mistakes, learn from them and try again."

Arturo C. Guevara

ACKNOWLEDGEMENTS

I thank Mireya, my wife, who always helps me when I start a new project to shape it, investigate and work until its completion, giving up some of the time we share so that I can carry out each new adventure.

To those friends who taught me that there are no limitations for coming from other latitudes and that the goals are always possible to achieve even if you are in a different environment from your origin.

To my children Eduardo and Ximena who always support me in any new initiative besides being great collaborators in research, review and sometimes translation.

To Isabel for her kind proofreading.

To those persons, who during this time in the USA have encouraged me to go ahead and work as hard as we did somewhere else.

I hope this book gives you the tools you need to be able to do business successfully, minimizing risks. The process walked and lived in its own flesh, it is embodied here and with sincerity, I can tell you that hundreds of hours of investigation will be avoided and the processes will become easier and faster, minimizing the possible mistakes that are normally made, by not having the command of the new legal framework economic, social, normally incurred. Follow this reference guide and try to reach your goals while achieving the American Dream.

Arturo C. Guevara
Business Consultant
Miami, Florida 2019
aguevara@usttg.com

CHAPTER ONE

Understanding the Scope

INTRODUCTION

This book will try to guide you on how to do the things in the right order, to be successful on your hiring process, right from the beginning. Steps to follow will help you to minimize your risks. Follow the process.

The United States and its 50 states, have different regulations. Some states are more flexible than others are but not all of them have the same labor legal system, as an example, Minimum Wages. Time is money and mistakes will have a cost in time. The process to hire employees differs from state to state. Florida is one of the states with the most flexible legal frame.

The first thing that you have to be aware of is what I am looking for. Am I looking for Administrative personnel? A top notch Professional or Executive? A floor plant worker to help in certain processes or somebody who can help my company to increase sales? Do I need him/her as a full time employee, temporary or as an Independent Contractor? Do they have to sign a Non-Disclosure Agreement or a Non-Compete Agreement? What do I want / expect from them? Do I have its Job Description and Responsibilities, well defined?

The process to hire a new employee will cost you money. Once you have them trained for the position, to let him leave will cost you more. To replace a full time employee will cost you more than twice the money you pay him/her as a salary and then you will go back to square one, having to train them again. Make the right decision and keep your staff motivated and they will go along with you and your business.

Hire the right people for the right position. Pay the employees the right salary and they will be there for long time. Underpaid workers will move away soon. Most of the time, people move for money and not in large sums but for cents on an hourly base. Provide them with the right tools to do their job well and you will minimize risks, for example, OSHA norms and procedures.

Follow the law and regulations. Keep a file for each worker and you will be safe.

Remember that it is a practical guide to hire employees. It does not replace the advice from Labor Lawyers.

CHAPTER TWO

Hiring Employees

INTERVIEWING

When interviewing it is important that you only ask questions that are reasonably related to the job in question. For example, asking questions about whether the applicant has had any traffic violations in the past five years is not necessary for someone applying for a desk job.

Similarly, employers should try to avoid questions that unintentionally pertain to the worker's protected status. For example, asking what years the worker attended high school or college seems innocent enough, however it reveals the worker's age, which is a protected status in the employment context.

PRE-EMPLOYMENT TESTING

Employers are allowed to require the worker to take a pre-employment test before a job offer is made. These tests are normally designed to test the workers skills in a particular area.

The test must meet the following criteria:
* The test must only measure essential job related abilities.
* The test must be required of all applicants for this position, regardless of disability status.
* The test must accurately reflect the applicant's achievement level or other relevant factors, and it may not reflect the applicant has impaired sensory, manual, or speaking skills except when those specific skills are being tested.
* The test must not be given for the purpose of discriminating against one of the protected classes.

OFFER OF EMPLOYMENT

A standard job offer should include the following details:
* Salary
* Benefits
* Position job title
* Name of the supervisor of the position
* Anticipated start date
* Other terms and conditions of employment

Be sure that the written employment contract has a clause stipulating that it supersedes all other oral/written agreements. This will protect your company from liability should there be a miscommunication between you and the new hire.

EMPLOYMENT AND CONTRACTS / AGREEMENTS
* Hire and Pay employees
* Building your Team / Benefits / Others
* Choose an in-house or external service for administering payroll
* Differences between Employee and Independent Contractors
* Non-Disclosure Agreement (NDA)
* Non-Compete Agreement (NCA)
* Recommendations about Employees files

HIRE AND PAY EMPLOYEES

If you are going to hire employees, before finding the right person for the job, you will need to create a plan for paying them. Follow these steps to set up payroll:

* Ensure new employees return a completed W-4 form
* Schedule pay periods to coordinate tax withholding for IRS
* Decide if you want independent contractors or an employee or both.
* Create a compensation plan for holiday, vacation and leave
* Decide who will manage your payroll system
* Know which records must stay on file and for how long
* Report payroll taxes as needed on quarterly and annual basis
* Choose an in-house or external service for administering payroll

The IRS maintains the Employer's Tax Guide, which provides guidance on all federal tax filing requirements that could apply to the obligations for your small business. Check with your state tax agency for employer filing stipulations.

HIRE EXTERNAL SERVICES FOR PAYROLL

Establish a basic payroll structure to help you hire employees. After that, manage them properly with a general understanding of state and federal labor laws but I would recommend you not to burden yourself with administrative chores. Find a company who does it for you. There are too many issues like details of payment, filing taxes, amongst other things.

BUILDING YOUR TEAM

BENEFITS FOR EMPLOYEES / RETAINING EMPLOYEES

Plan to offer employee benefits, as one of the best tools to keep employees or hire them. For most, benefits as Healthcare Insurance, Social Security and Workers comp, are really a matter to decide if I work independently or not. These items play a significant role in hiring and retaining employees.

THERE ARE SOME OTHER OPTIONAL EMPLOYEE BENEFITS

Your small businesses can offer a complete range of optional benefits to help attract and retain employees. Even if a benefit you offer is optional, check if it might still have to comply with certain laws if you choose to offer it. *For example*, businesses that offer group health plans must comply with federal laws, for which the Department of Labor hosts a guide. For detailed info, go to www.dol.gov

RETIREMENT PLANS are very popular as employee benefit. Consider offering an employer-sponsored plan like a 401k or a pension plan. The federal government offers a wide range of resources to aid small business owners in choosing their retirement plan and pension. For detailed info, go to https://webapps.dol.gov/

EMPLOYEE INCENTIVE PROGRAMS

Employee incentive programs can boost morale and create more draw for open positions: Common incentives such as stock options, flex time, wellness programs, corporate memberships and company events.

EMOTIONAL SALARY PROGRAM

What is the emotional salary? We talk of an emotional salary on referring to the perks companies offer their employees to improve their levels of job satisfaction without this actually meaning a pay increase. There are several issues related to Emotional Salary but the two most important are: the work setting and the attention given to the employee by management.

Emotional salary can contemplate as well:
* A good atmosphere at work
* Flexible hours
* The possibility of choosing when you take your holidays
* Remote working
* Company-provided training

Those are some of the aspects to bear in mind to increase motivation, since they have a strong impact on employee morale and therefore on their productivity.

Source: World Trade Center – Barcelona, Spain.
http://www.wtcbarcelona.com/en/news-wtcb/business-trends/892-emotional-salary

CHAPTER THREE

Employment and Federal Laws

HIRING EMPLOYEES AND LAWS
Laws, Regulations, Contracts types, NDA and NCA

EMPLOYMENT AND FEDERAL LAWS

MINIMUM WAGES
The Federal Law requires that most employees in the U.S be paid at least the federal minimum wage. There are certain States where the minimum wages are higher than the Federal ones. Then, you have to pay the employees the higher wage, as is the case of Florida, for all hours worked, or overtime pay at one and one-half of the regular rate for all hours worked after 40 hours in a workweek the law establishes that it applies for both: Salary Staff and hourly workers depending of their specific job duties, as well.

Federal Minimum Wage nationwide is **$7.25** per hour and overtime after 40 hours and not less than one and one-half times than regular pay rate after 40 hours of work a per week.
Florida minimum wage (2019) is **$8.46** per hour, therefore, in Florida you have to pay it as a minimum wage.
Source: www.dol.goc

PENALTIES ESTABLISHED BY THE U. S. DEPARTMENT OF LABOR

Civil Money Penalty Inflation Adjustments
Starting in 2016, agencies across the federal government must adjust their penalties for inflation each year. Below is a table that reflects the adjustments that have occurred for penalties under this statute.

Civil Money Penalty Inflation Adjustments

Type of Violation	Statutory Citation	CF Citation	Maximum Civil Monetary Penalty on / or before 1/23/2019	Maximum Civil Monetary Penalty on / or after 1/24/2019
Minimum Wage and Overtime: Repeated or willful violation of section 206 or 207.	29 USC 216(e)(2)	29 CFR 578.3(a)	$1,964	$2,014

Source: https://www.dol.gov/whd/ag/ag_fieldsan.htm#cmp

OCCUPATIONAL SAFETY AND HEALTH ACT

Occupational Safety and Health (OSH) Act - Requires employers to comply with occupational safety and health standards issued by the Occupational Safety and Health Administration (OSHA) and to provide employees with a workplace that is free from recognized hazards that are causing or likely to cause death or serious physical harm. The OSH Act is administered and enforced by OSHA.

Source: https://www.osha.gov/

Civil Money Penalty Inflation Adjustments

Type of Violation	Statutory Citation	CFR Citation	Maximum Civil Monetary Penalty on or before 1/23/2019	Maximum Civil Monetary Penalty on or after 1/24/2019
Failure to correct a violation for which a citation has been issued under section 9(a) of the OSH Act within the period permitted for the correction.	29 USC 666(d)	29 CFR 1903.15(d) (5)	$12,934	$13,260
Violation of the requirements of section 5 of the OSH Act, any standard, rule or order promulgated under section 6 of the OSH Act, or applicable regulations.	29 USC 666(c)	29 CFR 1903.15(d) (4)	$12,934	$13,260
Violation of any of the posting requirements, as prescribed under provisions of the OSH Act.	29 USC 666(i)	29 CFR 1903.15(d) (6)	$12,934	$13,260
Serious violation of the requirements of section 5 of the OSH Act, of any standard, rule, or order promulgated under section 6 of the OSH Act, or applicable regulations.	29 USC 666(b)	29 CFR 1903.15(d) (3)	$12,934	$13,260
Willful or repeated violation of the requirements of section 5 of the OSH Act, any standards, rules or orders promulgated under section 6 of the OSH Act, or applicable regulations.	29 USC 666(a)	29 CFR 1903.15(d) (1) and 29 CFR 1903.15(d) (2)	$129,336	$132,598

Source: https://www.dol.gov/whd/ag/ag_fieldsan.htm#cmp

THE AMERICAN WITH DISABILITIES ACT

Title I of the Americans with Disabilities Act of 1990 prohibits private employers, State and local governments, employment agencies and labor unions from discriminating against qualified individuals with disabilities in job application procedures, hiring, firing, advancement, compensation, job training, and other terms, conditions, and privileges of employment. The ADA covers employers with 15 or more employees, including State and local governments. It also applies to employment agencies and to labor organizations.

Source: www.ada.gov

FAMILY AND MEDICAL LEAVE

The **Family and Medical Leave** (FMLA) entitles eligible employees of covered employers to take unpaid, job-protected leave for specified family and medical reasons with continuation of group health insurance coverage under the same terms and conditions as if the employee had not taken leave. Eligible employees are entitled to:

15

Twelve workweeks of leave in a 12-month period for:

* the birth of a child and to care for the newborn child within one year of birth;
* the placement with the employee of a child for adoption or foster care and to care for the newly placed child within one year of placement;
* to care for the employee's spouse, child, or parent who has a serious health condition;
* a serious health condition that makes the employee unable to perform the essential functions of his or her job;
* any qualifying exigency arising out of the fact that the employee's spouse, son, daughter, or parent is a covered military member on "covered active duty;"

or

Twenty-six workweeks of leave during a single 12-month period to care for a covered service member with a serious injury or illness if the eligible employee is the service member's spouse, son, daughter, parent, or next of kin (military caregiver leave).

Note: FMLA applies for those business employing 50 or more employees.

Source: www.dol.gov

THE U. S. EQUAL EMPLOYMENT OPPORTUNITY COMMISSION (EEOC)
The EEOC Federal Laws Prohibiting Job Discrimination

These laws protect employees and job applicants against employment discrimination when it involves:

* Unfair treatment because of race, color, religion, sex (including pregnancy, gender identity, and sexual orientation), national origin, age (40 or older), disability or genetic information.
* Harassment by managers, co-workers, or others in the workplace, because of race, color, religion, sex (including pregnancy), national origin, age (40 or older), disability or genetic information.
* Denial of a reasonable workplace accommodation that the employee needs because of religious beliefs or disability.
* Retaliation because the employee complained about job discrimination, or assisted with a job discrimination investigation or lawsuit.

EQUAL PAY ACT (EPA)
* The EPA prohibits sex-based wage discrimination between men and women in the same establishment who perform jobs that require substantially equal skill, effort and responsibility under similar working conditions.

CHAPTER FOUR

Employment and Florida Laws

FLORIDA STATE EMPLOYMENT AND LAWS

- Florida Minimum Wage
- Worker's Compensation
- Child Labor
- Background Check

Florida minimum wage (2019) is **$8.46,** therefore, in Florida you have to pay it as a minimum wage.

Source: www.dol.goc

Penalty by the Florida State Constitution

See Section 24, Article X of the State Constitution and Section 448.110, Florida Statutes, establish the following:

"An employer found liable for intentionally violating minimum wage requirements is subject to a fine of $1,000 per violation, payable to the state. The Attorney General or other official designated by the Legislature may bring a civil action to enforce the minimum wage".

Source: http://www.floridajobs.org

If you want more information about Minimum Wage on the different states, go the following link: https://www.dol.gov/whd/minwage/america.htm#stateDetails

State Minimum Wage Laws

Minimum Wage Salaries in Florida from January 01, 2020.
Up to December 31st 2019 Florida´s minimum wage salary is $8.46 per hour but from January 01, 2002 it will go up to $8.56, base on the Florida's Minimum Wage Act. The increase is calculated by the Florida Department of Economic Opportunity and is based on the percentage increase in the Consumer Price Index for the South Region. This minimum wage salary in Florida is higher than the Federal minimum hourly wage which is $ 7.25. Tipped employees salary will $ 5.54 per hour from January 2020.

WORKERS COMPENSATION
Requires employers with four or more employees (full or part-time) to carry workers 'compensation coverage' for their employees; different requirements apply for construction and agriculture.
Source: www.myfloridacfo.com/division/wc

The Florida Workers Compensation statute states the following:

"440.015 Legislative intent.—It is the intent of the Legislature that the Workers' Compensation Law be interpreted so as *to assure the quick and efficient delivery of disability and medical benefits to an injured worker and to facilitate the worker's return to gainful reemployment at a reasonable cost to the employer.*"

The statute also states, "It is the specific intent of the Legislature that workers' compensation cases shall be decided on their merits."

Employers and employees alike base the workers' compensation system in Florida on a mutual renunciation of common-law rights and defenses. In addition, it is the intent of the Legislature that the facts in a workers' compensation case are not to be interpreted liberally in favor of either the rights of the injured worker or the rights of the employer.

Additionally, the legislature hereby declares that disputes concerning the facts in workers' compensation cases are not to be given a broad liberal construction in favor of the employee on the one hand or of the employer on the other hand, and the laws pertaining to workers' compensation are to be construed in accordance with the basic principles of statutory construction and not liberally in favor of either employee or employer.
Source: www.myfloridacfo.com/division/wc

CHILD LABOR
Workers under 18 cannot work in certain hazardous occupation, including excavation, electrical work, roofing and mining, or around explosives, toxic or radioactive substances or dangerous equipment. Additional occupations are banned for children ages 14-15. Minors cannot work during school hours without an exception.
Source: floridatrend.com

BACKGROUND CHECK
Private citizens or companies may request a state-only criminal history record check of an individual through the Florida Department of Law Enforcement
Source: www.fdle.stte.fl.us

You can get through private corps, to check some people's credit and legal issues. To do so, the people you want to check, have to sign a written authorization allowing you to ask for their credit and legal records. You have to protect their data.

SUMMARY OF THE MAJOR LAWS OF THE DEPARTMENT OF LABOR

* Wages & Hours
* Workplace Safety & Health
* Workers' Compensation
* Employee Benefits
* Unions & Their Members
* Employee Protection
* Uniformed Services Employment and Reemployment Rights Act
* Employee Polygraph Protection Act
* Garnishment of Wages
* The Family and Medical Leave Act
* Veterans' Preference
* Government Contracts, Grants, or Financial Aid
* Migrant & Seasonal Agricultural Workers
* Mine Safety & Health
* Construction
* Transportation
* Plant Closings & Layoffs
* Posters
* Related Agencies

The Department of Labor (DOL) administers and enforces more than 180 federal laws. These mandates and the regulations that implement them cover many workplace activities for about 10 million employers and 125 million workers.

CHAPTER FIVE

Types of Agreements

NON-DISCLOSURE AGREEMENT - DEFINITION

A non-disclosure agreement is a legal contract in which the parties involved agree to keep the information included private. This type of contract creates a confidential relationship between the parties, and protects the confidential or proprietary information (2) outlined in the agreement, as breaching a non-disclosure agreement generally subjects the party to severe civil penalties. To explore this concept, consider the following non-disclosure agreement definition.

NON-COMPETE AGREEMENT - DEFINITION
NON-COMPETE AGREEMENT (NCA)-COVENANT NOT TO COMPETE

A term used in contract law, a **"covenant not to compete"** is an agreement in which an individual, usually an employee, agrees not to work for the other party's competition in a specified geographical area for a specified length of time. Also referred to as a "non-compete clause," or "non-compete agreement," this type of legal agreement is commonly used in employment contracts and in contracts for the sale of a business. To explore this concept, consider the following covenant not to compete definition.

NON-DISCLOSURE AGREEMENT

A non-disclosure agreement
(1) is a legal contract in which the parties involved agree to keep the information included private. This type of contract creates a confidential relationship between the parties, and protects the confidential or proprietary information

(2) outlined in the agreement, as breaching a non-disclosure agreement generally subjects the party to severe civil penalties. To explore this concept, consider the following non-disclosure agreement definition.

- *Definition of Non-Disclosure Agreement*
Noun:
A contract in which one or more parties promise to keep information confidential, and not disclose it to any other party without proper authorization.

(2) Definition of Proprietary Information
Noun:
Information that a company or other entity wishes to keep confidential.

WHAT IS A NON-DISCLOSURE AGREEMENT?

A non-disclosure agreement is a legal contract used to protect information that must be shared by one party to another in order to do business, but which must be kept confidential or secret. Also referred to as an "NDA," "confidentiality (3) agreement," or "proprietary information agreement," such a contract outlines the nature of the confidential information, without disclosing it specifically. The contract restricts one party involved from sharing the other party's information with outside parties without first having proper authorization.

NDAs are most commonly used in businesses when the need to establish a confidential relationship with employees or contractors arises. Such information may include trade secrets, proprietary information, client lists, database information, or any other information considered vital to the business.

CONFIDENTIALITY - DEFINITION
NOUN
* Something told in confidence, or in secret
* The state of knowledge being held in confidence
* The state of trusting another individual with private affairs or secrets

EXAMPLE OF NON-DISCLOSURE AGREEMENT SITUATION
Richard is hired on as a chemist at a high-tech pharmacological laboratory. The research at the laboratory and the formulas used in its experiments and drugs are kept secret to prevent other drug companies from obtaining any of the information and duplicating their work. As a condition of employment, Richard is asked to sign a non-disclosure agreement that requires him to keep any information pertaining to the work at the lab secret.

Once Richard signs the company's non-disclosure agreement, he is legally bound to keep all of their information private. Sharing any of the information could result, not only in Richard's termination, but also in a civil lawsuit for breach of contract.

STANDARD NON-DISCLOSURE AGREEMENT
In general, a standard non-disclosure agreement is used to ensure a party does not share confidential information that is disclosed to him in a business transaction, or in the course of his employment. A standard non-disclosure agreement outlines the information that should be protected, which varies depending on the situation. The Small Business Association offers information for businesses, including the use of non-disclosure agreements.

BASIC ELEMENTS ON A NDA
There are five basic elements that should be part of any standard non-disclosure agreement. These include:

THE CONFIDENTIAL INFORMATION – The non-disclosure agreement should clearly spell out the information that is to be protected, to prevent any misunderstanding or questions about the confidentiality. Not all information presented in a non-disclosure agreement is confidential, as there is some standard information that pertains to most contracts. The actual confidential information is not usually listed in the agreement, only a description of the type of information.

EXCLUSIONS FROM CONFIDENTIAL INFORMATION – Nearly all non-disclosure agreements contain exclusions from the confidential information. In basic terms, the party has no duty to protect the information that is excluded from the agreement. Law excludes information discovered or created by the receiving party prior to any involvement with the disclosing party.

OBLIGATIONS AND DUTIES – A non-disclosure agreement should clearly state the duties and obligations of all parties. In most jurisdictions, a receiving party's obligation is not limited to personally keeping the information confidential, but he cannot cause or induce others to acquire the information inappropriately either.

TIME PERIODS – Most non-disclosure agreements have a time period for which they are enforceable. The agreement is normally in effect during the entire course of the parties' involvement, such as the receiving party's employment, plus a specified number of years following termination of employment or other relationship.

OTHER PROVISIONS – A non-disclosure agreement may include provisions based on the needs of the company. These are often referred to as "boilerplate provisions," and are included at the end of the contract. These provisions generally include which state's laws govern the contract, how disputes will be handled, and consequences for failing to abide by the contract.

EMPLOYEE NON-DISCLOSURE AGREEMENT
Many companies use employee non-disclosure agreements to protect the company's information or trade secrets. An employee non-disclosure agreement outlines the company's policies regarding their proprietary information to which the employee has access during the course of his employment. This type of NDA prohibits employees from unauthorized use, and sharing, of such information as:

* Customer lists
* Financial information
* Business plans
* Business operations
* Business models
* Others stated on the agreement

Before a person signs an employee non-disclosure agreement, he should read it carefully and make sure he understands all of the information presented. Such agreements are often presented during the hiring process, and, if the employee refuses to sign, the employer can refuse to hire him. Some companies include the non-disclosure agreement in the employee handbook (*).

(*) EMPLOYEE HANDBOOK - DEFINITION
NOUN
A handbook or manual provided to employees by their employers, which outlines important company information, policies, procedures, and job descriptions.

MUTUAL NON-DISCLOSURE AGREEMENT
When two or more parties plan to share confidential information, which is commonly done between business entities, or between entrepreneurs collaborating on a new project, a mutual non-disclosure agreement protects the proprietary information of both parties. Also referred to as a "bilateral non-disclosure agreement," a mutual non-disclosure agreement binds all parties to keep the specified information secret.

EXAMPLE OF MUTUAL NON-DISCLOSURE AGREEMENT
Mary and George decide to go into business together, using Mary's new clothing designs and George's innovative production techniques to launch a new line of clothes. Both Mary and George want to protect their ideas, while sharing them in order to do business together. A mutual non-disclosure agreement outlines the types of information each party brings to the business, which must be kept confidential. It may also specify that any information created or discovered during the course of the business relationship must also be kept secret.

BREACHING A NON-DISCLOSURE AGREEMENT

When a person signs a non-disclosure agreement, he has entered into a legally binding contract to keep the specified information private. Breaching a non-disclosure agreement is a serious issue that can result in large-scale legal consequences. The laws governing confidential information and trade secrets are spelled out in the Uniform Trade Secrets Act. Information protected by law includes patterns, drawings, devices, programs, techniques, and much more.

BREACHING A NDA

When a disclosing party believes his non-disclosure agreement has been breached, he should review the original contract to determine the remedies available to him, as well as any processes specified. The next step is investigating the breach to ensure there is concrete evidence to explain how the information was leaked. Once such evidence has been obtained, the non-breaching party may file a civil lawsuit against the breaching party.

Normally, the remedy available to the wronged party will be in the form of monetary damages awarded by the court, if his case is proven. In some cases, the court may issue an order barring the breaching party from further disclosing protected information. This is referred to as an "injunction."

EXAMPLE OF BREACH OF NON-DISCLOSURE AGREEMENT

In 2003, Wall Street trader Lauren Brenner was inspired to start a physical fitness studio based on military boot camp-style programs. She visited Fort Knox on several occasions to learn and design materials she would use. After studying the program, she opened Pure Power Boot Camp in New York City. The studio used military colors and obstacles designed to fit an indoor space.

The studio employed a unique method of payment by clientele, in which no membership fee was charged, but clients were referred to as "recruits" who signed up for returning "tours of duty." Brenner hired former marines as instructors to drill the recruits, two of which became her most trusted employees.

The studio was successful from the beginning, and Brenner planned to expand the operation. Her employees signed an employee agreement which contained non-disclosure, non-compete, and non-solicitation (5) provisions. After opening a second location in Manhattan, Brenner invited one of the two top marines to become a partner. He refused, claiming he did not have the money to invest.

In reality, the two instructors were planning to open their own boot camp gym with investments from their girlfriends. They leased a space 15 blocks from Brenner's facility, and stole her Pure Power studio documents from her office, and destroyed their own employee agreements. The stolen documents included Pure Power Bootcamp business plan, its startup information, and its client list.

Before she learned about the stolen documents, Brenner got into an argument with one of the drill instructors and fired him. The other drill instructor promptly quit. The men used the stolen documents to open their own Warrior Fitness Boot Camp, going too far as to email Pure Power's clients in an attempt to get them to switch to their gym.

When Brenner learned the men had stolen her confidential information to form their own business, she filed a lawsuit seeking an injunction against the competing business. While the court denied her request for an injunction, finding that the non-compete agreement was not enforceable. The judge did order the men to return the stolen materials, and to alter their dress code for their clients.

The case was then taken to federal court where the parties eventually had a bench trial. This court found that the two men had clearly breached the non-disclosure agreement portions of their employee contracts, and ordered the men to forfeit about $96,000 in salaries. It also awarded the men to pay punitive damages in the amount of $150,000 for their "egregious" betrayals of the plaintiff's trust.

(*) SOLICITATION DEFINITION
NOUN
* The act of seeking something by persuasion or entreaty
* A persistent petition or request
* The act of enticing another to commit a criminal offense or illegal act
* The act of accosting someone for something in exchange for payment

RELATED LEGAL TERMS AND ISSUES

CIVIL LAWSUIT – A lawsuit brought about in court when one person claims to have suffered a loss due to the actions of another person.

CONTRACT – An agreement between two or more parties in which a promise is made to do or provide something in return for a valuable benefit.

DAMAGES – A monetary award in compensation for a financial loss, loss of or damage to personal or real property, or an injury.

DEFENDANT – A party against whom a lawsuit has been filed in civil court, or who has been accused of, or charged with, a crime or offense.

LEGALLY BINDING – An agreement that is written and enforceable by law.

OBLIGATION – A promise or contract that is legally binding; the act of binding or obliging oneself, as in a contract.

PLAINTIFF – A person who brings a legal action against another person or entity, such as in a civil lawsuit, or criminal proceedings.

PUNITIVE DAMAGES – Money awarded to the injured party above and beyond their actual damages. Punitive damages may be awarded in cases where the defendant's actions concerning the case are malicious, or so reckless as to give a reasonable person pause. Punitive damages, also referred to as "exemplary damages," are ordered for the purpose of punishing the wrongdoer for outrageous misconduct in a civil matter.

Source: Non-Disclosure Agreements, from Legal Dictionary.
https://legaldictionary.net/non-disclosure-agreement/

NON-COMPETE AGREEMENT (NCA)-COVENANT NOT TO COMPETE

A term used in contract law, a **"covenant not to compete** (*)" is an agreement in which an individual, usually an employee, agrees not to work for the other party's competition in a specified geographical area for a specified length of time. Also referred to as a "non-compete clause," or "non-compete agreement," this type of legal agreement is commonly used in employment contracts and in contracts for the sale of a business. To explore this concept, consider the following covenant not to compete definition.

(*) COVENANT NOT TO COMPETE - DEFINITION
NOUN
A promise made by an employee, or the seller of a business, not to compete in the same type of business in the same area for a certain time period.

PURPOSE OF A COVENANT NOT TO COMPETE
The purpose of a covenant not to compete is to protect a business interest by limiting competition. An employer hiring an employee that is a professional in a specialized field may seek to limit the ability of a competitor to hire that employee in the event he leaves the company. Alternatively, an individual seeking to purchase a business may use a non-compete clause to prevent the seller from opening a new, similar business in the same area for a specified length of time.

COVENANT NOT TO COMPETE FORM
While many companies hire attorneys to prepare their ***non-compete agreements***, an individual or entity may find a covenant not to compete form that suits their needs online.

INFORMATION THAT SHOULD BE INCLUDED ON EVERY COVENANT NOT TO COMPETE FORM INCLUDES:
* The full names of each party to the agreement
* Date the agreement is made
* The specifics of what business or activities are not to be in competition with the employer or business
* What remedy will be available to either party in the event the agreement is breached
* Legality of a Covenant Not to Compete

While most states recognize covenant not to compete agreements in some form, some states prohibit them except in specific limited circumstances. Non-compete clauses are commonly used in employment contracts for popular radio and TV personalities. This prevents, for example, a well-liked radio morning show personality, or TV anchorperson from leaving their station and going directly to work for a competitor, taking their fans with them.

States that restrict the use of covenant not to compete agreements often look at the scope and function of such an agreement in determining whether it is enforceable. Important considerations in determining the legality of a covenant not to compete agreement include whether the clause is reasonably necessary to protect legitimate business interests, such as trade secrets, and whether the agreement unnecessarily restricts the employee's ability to earn a living.

WHICH STATES DO NOT ALLOW NON-COMPETE AGREEMENTS?
A few **states**, such as California, Montana, North Dakota, and Oklahoma, totally ban **non-compete agreements** for employees, or prohibit all **non-compete agreements** except in limited circumstances.

RELATED LEGAL TERMS AND ISSUES
CLAUSE – A section of a legal document that relates to a particular point or issue.
SCOPE – Relevant range of authority or practice, or range of control through a contract.
FUNCTION – The purpose for which something is designed or exists.
TRADE SECRETS – Designs, practices, processes, commercial methods, techniques, or information that is not generally known by others, which gives a business an advantage over competitors.

INJUNCTION – A court order preventing an individual or entity from beginning or continuing an action. (source: https://legaldictionary.net/covenant-not-to-compete/)

States law rules regarding non-compete agreements

Increasingly, states are restricting or barring entirely the use of non-compete agreements, especially for "low-wage" workers. Here is a roundup of some recent legislation that may affect your business.

- **CALIFORNIA.** Non-compete agreements cannot be enforced in this state.
- **IDAHO.** Employers can have non-compete agreements with key employees, but they must be reasonable in duration, geographic area, and type of employment.
- **ILLINOIS.** Employers cannot have a low-wage worker (someone earning less than $13 per hour) sign a non-compete agreement.
- **MAINE.** Employers cannot have a worker earning an hourly wage at or below 300% of the federal poverty level. What's more, the worker must be given three days before signing an agreement and it cannot take effect before the employee has worked at least one year or six months after signing, whichever is later. The rule is effective on September 1, 2019.
- **MASSACHUSETTS.** Employers cannot have a non-compete agreement with a non-exempt employee (i.e., someone who is hourly and not in management). Where non-compete agreements can be used, they must be limited in scope (no more than a one-year term, reasonable geographic area). The rule applies to agreements entered into on or after October 1, 2018.
- **NEW HAMPSHIRE.** Employers cannot have a worker earning an hourly rate less than or equal to 200% of the federal minimum wage (which would be $14.50 at the present) sign a non-compete agreement. The rule is effective on September 1, 2019.
- **UTAH.** Employers can have a non-compete agreement, but it cannot run longer than one year.

(Source: Barbara Weltman - Big Ideas for Small Business - Analyses what is happening in some states nowadays.)

FLORIDA – NON-COMPETE LITIGATION

As commented by the Mavrick Law web page, Non-compete contracts contravene Florida's general public and statutory policy encouraging free enterprise and competition. They are allowed as an exception to that policy under certain circumstances.

Source: https://www.mavricklaw.com

"Valid Non-Compete Agreements under Florida Law can Prohibit Only "Unfair Competition" Not "Ordinary Competition"

Florida Statutes section 542.335 governs restrictive covenants, also called "non-compete" covenants. Section 542.335(1)(a), Florida Statutes, requires that "(t)he person seeking enforcement of a restrictive covenant shall plead and prove one or more legitimate business interests justifying the restrictive covenant." Case law interpreting the statute states that "ordinary competition" is not prohibited, and the statute allows enforcement of a non-compete covenant only when there is "unfair competition." In White v. Mederi

Caretenders Visiting Services of Southeast, Florida, LLC, 226 So. 3d 774,784–85 (Fla. 2017), the Florida Supreme Court explained in pertinent part:

…[A] "legitimate business interest" is an identifiable business asset that constitutes or represents an investment by the proponent of the restriction such that, if that asset were misappropriated by a competitor (i.e., taken without compensation), its use in competition against its former owner would be "unfair competition." Put another way, a "legitimate business interest" is a business asset that, if misappropriated, would give its new owner an unfair competitive advantage over its former owner …Section 542.335 does not protect covenants 'whose sole purpose is to prevent competition per se' because those contracts are void against public policy. Colucci, 918 So.2d at 440. For an employer to be entitled to protection, 'there must be special facts present over and above ordinary competition' such that, absent a non-competition agreement, 'the employee would gain an unfair advantage in future competition with the employer.'

LEGITIMATE BUSINESSES INTERESTS SUPPORTING A FLORIDA NON-COMPETE CONTRACT

Florida's non-compete statute specifically states that a non-compete "not supported by a legitimate business interest is unlawful and is void and unenforceable." The meaning of what is a "legitimate business interest" has been the source of a great deal of litigation. Florida's non-compete statute does not define all possible "legitimate business interests," but the statute does state that the following will qualify as legitimate to enforce a non-compete:

- "Trade secrets" as defined by separate Florida statute;
- Valuable confidential business or professional information that does not otherwise qualify as trade secrets;
- Substantial relationships with specific prospective or existing customers, patients, or clients;
- Customer, patient, or client goodwill; and
- Extraordinary or specialized training.

WHAT IS YOUR ALTERNATIVE?
As described by **Barbara Weltman, Big Ideas for Small Business,**
"While you may not want or be able to make an employee sign a non-compete agreement to keep him/her from working for a competitor or starting a competing business, you can still protect your company with a nondisclosure (or confidentiality) agreement. This type of contract bars employees from using a company's confidential information, including customer lists, price lists, and other trade secrets and proprietary information, outside of the company. These agreements are enforceable in all states provided they are drafted properly.

Best practice: Have an employee sign a nondisclosure agreement when starting employment with you. Some companies include the agreement in their employee manual. Whether or not you do this, it is a good idea to have the employee sign a separate statement acknowledging that he/she has read the confidentiality agreement and understands what it means. And be sure you have your agreement reviewed by an employment law attorney."

CHAPTER SIX

Working Relationship

DIFFERENCE BETWEEN EMPLOYEES AND INDEPENDENT CONTRACTORS – DEFINITIONS.

"If an employer-employee relationship exists (regardless of what the relationship is called), you are not an independent contractor and your earnings are generally not subject to Self-Employment Tax." www.irs.gov

INDEPENDENT CONTRACTOR - IRS DEFINITION

INDEPENDENTS CONTRACTORS are self-employed, work independently, and provide services to other businesses, and they are not controlled directly by the employer. An independent contractor operates under a separate business name from your company and invoices for work completed. Independent contractors can sometimes qualify as employees in a legal sense. Keep an eye and avoid to have your independent contractor considered an employee. The Equal Employment Opportunity Commission created a guide for making the determination. www.sba.goc./ www.eeoc.gov.

EMPLOYEES are controlled by an employer (what will be done and how it will be done). This applies even if you are given freedom of action. What matters is that the employer has the legal right to control the details of how the services are performed.

Distinguishing between employees and independent contractors can impact your bottom line, as this affects how you withhold taxes and avoid costly legal consequences. Learn the differences before hiring your first employee....
If your independent contractor is discovered to meet the legal definition of employee, you may need to pay back taxes and penalties, provide benefits, and reimburse for wages stipulated under the Fair Labor Standards Act. www.dol.gov.

If your independent contractor is discovered to meet the legal definition of employee, you may need to pay back taxes and penalties, provide benefits, and reimburse for wages stipulated under the Fair Labor Standards Act. www.dol.gov.

HOW TO DETERMINE IF SOMEONE IS AND INDEPENDENT CONTRACTOR.

In determining whether the person providing service is an employee or an independent contractor, all information that provides evidence of the degree of control and independence must be considered.

COMMON LAW RULES

The IRS applies the Common Law Rules to determine if someone is an Employee or Independent Contractor. Facts that provide evidence of the degree of control and independence fall into three categories:

Behavioral: Does the company control or have the right to control what the worker does and how the worker does his or her job?

Financial: Are the business aspects of the worker's job controlled by the payer? (these include things like how worker is paid, whether expenses are reimbursed, who provides tools/supplies, etc.)

Type of Relationship: Are there written contracts or employee type benefits (i.e., pension plan, insurance, vacation pay, etc.)? Will the relationship continue and is the work performed a key aspect of the business?

INDEPENDENT CONTRACTORS

IRS applies the Common Law Rules to determine if someone is an Employee or Independent Contractor.

COMMON LAW RULES
Facts that provide evidence of the degree of control and independence fall into three categories:

* **Behavioral:** Does the company control or have the right to control what the worker does and how the worker does his or her job?

* **Financial:** Are the business aspects of the worker's job controlled by the payer? (these include things like how worker is paid, whether expenses are reimbursed, who provides tools/supplies, etc.)

* **Type of Relationship:** Are there written contracts or employee type benefits (i.e., pension plan, insurance, vacation pay, etc.)? Will the relationship continue and is the work performed a key aspect of the business?

INDEPENDENT CONTRACTOR OR EMPLOYEE?

BEHAVIORAL CONTROL refers to facts that show whether there is a right to direct or control how the worker does the work. A worker is an employee when the business has the right to direct and control the worker. The business does not have to actually direct or control the way the work is done —as long as the employer has the right to direct and control the work.
The behavioral control factors fall into the categories of:

* Type of instructions given
* Degree of instruction
* Evaluation systems
* Training

TYPES OF INSTRUCTIONS GIVEN
An employee is generally subject to the business's instructions about when, where, and how to work. All of the following are examples of types of instructions about how to do work.

* When and where to do the work
* What tools or equipment to use
* What workers to hire or to assist with the work
* Where to purchase supplies and services
* What work must be performed by a specified individual
* What order or sequence to follow when performing the work

29

DEGREE OF INSTRUCTION

Degree of Instruction means that the more detailed the instructions, the more control the business exercises over the worker. More detailed instructions indicate that the worker is an employee. Less detailed instructions reflect less control, indicating that the worker is more likely an independent contractor.

NOTE: The amount of instruction needed varies among different jobs. Even if no instructions are given, sufficient behavioral control may exist if the employer has the right to control how the work results are achieved. A business may lack the knowledge to instruct some highly specialized professionals; in other cases, the task may require little or no instruction. The key consideration is whether the business has retained the right to control the details of a worker's performance or instead has given up that right.

EVALUATION SYSTEM

If an evaluation system measures the details of how the work is performed then, these factors would point to an employee.

If the evaluation system measures just the outcome then, this can point to either an independent contractor or an employee.

TRAINING

If the business provides the worker with training on how to do the job, this indicates that the business wants the job done in a particular way. This is strong evidence that the worker is an employee. Periodic or on-going training about procedures and methods is even stronger evidence of an employer-employee relationship. However, independent contractors ordinarily use their own methods.

FINANCIAL control refers to facts that show whether or not the business has the right to control the economic aspects of the worker's job. The financial control factors fall into the categories of:

*   Significant investment
*   Unreimbursed expenses
*   Opportunity for profit or loss
*   Services available to the market
*   Method of payment

SIGNIFICANT INVESTMENT

An independent contractor often has a significant investment in the equipment he or she uses in working for someone else. However, in many occupations, such as construction, workers spend thousands of dollars on the tools and equipment they use and are still considered to be employees. There is no precise amount of dollars that needs to be spent for a business to meet the test of. Furthermore, a significant investment is not necessary for independent contractor status, as some types of work simply do not require large expenditures.

UNREIMBURSED EXPENSES

Independent contractors are more likely to have unreimbursed expenses than are employees. Fixed ongoing costs that are incurred regardless of whether work is currently being performed are especially important. However, employees may also incur unreimbursed expenses in connection with the services that they perform for their business.

OPPORTUNITY FOR PROFIT OR LOSS

The opportunity to make a profit or loss is another important factor. If a worker has a significant investment in the tools and equipment used and if the worker has unreimbursed expenses, the worker has a greater opportunity to lose money (i.e., their expenses will exceed their income from the work). Having the possibility of incurring a loss indicates that the worker is an independent contractor.

SERVICES AVAILABLE TO THE MARKET

An independent contractor is generally free to seek out business opportunities. Independent contractors often advertise, maintain a visible business location, and are available to work in the relevant market.

METHOD OF PAYMENT

An employee is generally guaranteed a regular wage amount for an hourly, weekly, or other period of time. This usually indicates that a worker is an employee, even when the wage or salary is supplemented by a commission. An independent contractor is usually paid by a flat fee for the job. However, it is common in some professions, such as law, to pay independent contractors hourly.

TYPE OF RELATIONSHIP refers to facts that show how the worker and business perceive their relationship to each other.

The factors, for the type of relationship between two parties, generally fall into the categories of:

* Written contracts
* Employee benefits
* Permanency of the relationship
* Services provided as key activity of the business

WRITTEN CONTRACTS

Although a contract may state that the worker is an employee or an independent contractor, this is not sufficient to determine the worker's status. The IRS is not required to follow a contract stating that the worker is an independent contractor, responsible for paying his or her own self-employment tax. How the parties work together determines whether the worker is an employee or an independent contractor.

EMPLOYEE BENEFITS

Employee benefits include things like insurance, pension plans, paid vacation, sick days, and disability insurance. Businesses generally do not grant these benefits to independent contractors. However, the lack of these types of benefits does not necessarily mean the worker is an independent contractor.

PERMANENCY OF THE RELATIONSHIP

If you hire a worker with the expectation that the relationship will continue indefinitely, rather than for a specific project or period, this is generally considered evidence that the intent was to create an employer-employee relationship.

SERVICES PROVIDED AS KEY ACTIVITY OF THE BUSINESS

If a worker provides services that are a key aspect of the business, it is more likely that the business will have the right to direct and control his or her activities. For example, if a law firm hires an attorney, it is likely that it will present the attorney's work as its own and would have the right to control or direct that work. This would indicate an employer-employee relationship.

Employee or Independent Contractor

Employee / Intern

- Works exclusively for the company
- Company provides tools
- Company controls duties
- Company sets working hours
- Worker must perform services
- Worker has pension / group benefits
- Worker gets paid vacation
- Company pays expenses
- Worker is paid salary or hourly wage

Independent Contractor

- May work for other companies
- Worker provides tools
- Worker decides how the task is completed
- Worker sets own working hours
- Worker may hire someone else to complete the job
- Worker does not get benefits
- Worker gets no paid vacation, and has no restrictions on time off.
- Worker pays own expenses
- Worker is paid by the job on a predetermined basis

Contracted for specific project or time period	Works on ongoing basis and may be terminated at will
Decides when and where to work	Has required work schedule and location
Determines how to do work, process steps, and what tools are utilized	Is told how to perform work, in what order, and particular tools to use
Does not need or receive skills training	May be trained and instructed
Does not attend frequent meetings or give regular reports	May attend frequent meetings and give regular reports
Performs work requiring specialized skills that is not the client's primary service	May perform work that is a business' primary service
Negotiates and sets own rates, including fixed price amounts	Paid hourly wage or salary governed by minimum wage and overtime laws
Provides own tools and equipment, is responsible for own costs and expenses, and bears risk of loss	Reimbursed for all expenses needed for work
Markets services to public on Upwork or otherwise and works with multiple clients	May work full-time and exclusively
May delegate tasks to others	Must personally perform their work

STATUTORILY PROTECTED GROUPS

ACTIONS TO AVOID DURING AN INDEPENDENT CONTRACTOR ENGAGEMENT

* While working with any independent contractor, clients should be careful not to do
* any of the following:
* Require work not specified in an agreed contract
* Set the work location or work hours
* Provide tools or equipment
* Train on skills needed to do the work
* Specify process steps or work methods
* Give detailed instruction on how to do the work
* Schedule regular or frequent meetings or status reports
* Prohibit delegating tasks to subcontractors or employees
* Preclude working for other clients
* Specify the work you need done and any deadlines, but otherwise respect a freelance professional's independence at all times.

CHAPTER SEVEN

E-Verify

WHAT IS E-VERIFY?

Basically, E-Verify is an online system run by U. S. Citizenship and Immigration Services to help employers determine employee work eligibility. It is made to work simply with the **Form I-9**, a mandatory employee eligibility form.

IS IT MANDATORY TO USE E-VERIFY?

Since 1996, **E-Verify** has been voluntary for most employers. ... Although it is not currently **required** at a federal level, many states have laws that either require or encourage some employers to **use E-Verify** including: Arizona and Mississippi: **Required** (all employers)

If your business hires employees, you should know about E-Verify. The federal program tries to ensure employers that their new hires are eligible to work in the U. S. It is potentially relevant for all employers, and even mandatory for some. So exactly what is E-Verify and how does it work?

WHAT DOES E-VERIFY CHECKS?

Once you are signed up, you can add the information from an employee's **Form I-9** and the system will compare that information with records that are available to various federal government agencies, like the Department of Homeland Security and the Social Security Administration. This essentially gives you a simple way to verify whether or not a new hire is legally allowed to be employed in the U. S.

The program launched back in 1996 as a strictly voluntary program. DHS eventually started requiring federal contractors and vendors to enroll in the program back in 2007. It is still not required for all businesses on the federal level, though there have been talks of doing so. However, many states do have requirements in place for certain businesses.

WHO CAN USE E-VERIFY?

E-Verify is open to all U. S. employers. You can simply sign up on the website and add some basic information about your company to become a registered employer.

However, it is not a mandatory program for most employers. The exception is businesses that have federal contracts or subcontracts or want to apply for them. About 20 states also require at least some employers to use E-Verify. However, most of those mandates relate to government contractors and not private employers. Check with your state legislature if you are unsure about your specific requirements.

E-VERIFY OVERVIEW.

E-Verify is an Internet-based system that compares information from your **Form I-9**, Employment Eligibility Verification, to U.S. Department of Homeland Security (DHS) and Social Security Administration (SSA) records to confirm that you are authorized to work in the United States

E-Verify is a Web-based service that helps employers determine whether their newly hired employees are authorized to work in the United States. The new search tool replaces the lists of employers and federal contractors previously found in our E-Verify website.

E-Verify is an Internet-based system that compares information from your **Form I-9**, Employment Eligibility Verification, to U.S. Department of Homeland Security (DHS) and Social Security Administration (SSA) records to confirm that you are authorized to work in the United States.

Thereafter, DHS designated E-Verify "as the electronic employment eligibility verification system that all federal contractors must use as required by the amended Executive Order 12989".

E-Verify is a voluntary program for most employers, but mandatory for some, such as employers with federal contracts or subcontracts that contain the Federal Acquisition Regulation (FAR) E-Verify clause and employers in certain states that have legislation that mandates the use of E-Verify for some or all employers.

While E-Verify is generally voluntary, some states require employers to use E-Verify, and it is mandatory for some federal government contracts. It can eliminate "No Match letters" from the SSA notifying an employer that an employee's reported social security number does not match government records.

WHAT STATES REQUIRE E-VERIFY 2019?
* E-Verify States Map
* Florida
* Indiana
* Missouri
* Nebraska
* Oklahoma
* Pennsylvania
* Texas

E-VERIFY https://www.e-verify.gov/

CHAPTER EIGHT

Workers Files – Documents required

EMPLOYEE FILE
In many Federal and State, Labor Laws apply to certain sizes of companies only, such as those with 15 employees or more. However, it is recommended that small business owners do their best to follow Federal and State Labor Laws, regardless of size, in order to be supportive of your employees and maintain a strong reputation as a business owner

Every employee must have a file. The file must have the following documents:
* Signed Job Offer Letter
* Employee Personal Data Form
* Job Description and Responsibilities
* Background Check Authorization form signed
* W2 Tax Form
* Form I-9 and Supporting Documents
* Direct Deposit Authorization Form
* Federal W-4 Form
* Employee Handbook receipt signed
* Training receipt signed
* Company Worker's Compensation Insurance Policy Forms
* Company Health Insurance Policy Forms
* Disability Self-Identification Form (if business is done with government)
* Company Non-Disclosure Agreement (if applicable)
* An a Non-Compete Agreement (in some cases)

All employers in Florida must have the following poster:
* Employers in Florida are required to display both Federal and State Employment Posters.
* Uniformed Services Employment and Reemployment Right CCT (users) Poster
* Family and Medical Leave Act (FMLA) Poster
* Fair Labor Standards Act (FLSA) Minimum Wage Poster
* "Equal Employment Opportunity Is The Law" Poster
* Job Safety and Health: it's the law Poster
* Florida Law Prohibits Discrimination Poster
* RT-83 Florida Reemployment Assistance Program Law Poster

EMPLOYERS MUST COMPLY WITH FLORIDA STATE EMPLOYMENT STANDARDS

Florida Payroll Tax and Reporting Requirements
* Report new employees within 20 days of start of their work date with a Report of New Employee(s)
* File both a Quarterly Contribution Return and Report of Wages (RT 6)
* Deposit and report federal employment taxes to the IRS by following IRS procedures for payroll reporting and payment

- You should also check with your City and County to see if they have any other requirements for the hiring of new employees and any employment standards in addition to the state-wide requirements.

JOB OFFER

If a potential candidate successfully went through an interview process, you should send him/her a "Job Offer".

A Job Offer is a letter of employment intended to define the terms of employment, where the employer states exactly what the job is about and what is expect from accepting the role. You need to be careful in their drafting of them.
All Job offers should have an expiring date. It is better not to have a signed back confirmation letter from the candidate and add a note saying that you expect him in a specific date.

In a Job Letter, never use terms as Guaranteed, as it can be considering a contract. Is better to use terms like "Not Guaranteed" if you want to describe a special issue but conditioned to results or job performance.
Example: If the candidate you are sending the Job Letter will get commissions out based on sales objectives, indicate it but you should add the following: "Commissions are not guaranteed," as they depend on Sales Objectives.
Review the wording carefully to ensure that only what is intended is set forth in the offer letter.

Therefore, a Job Offer letter, is a formal confirmation of the Job opportunity and should indicates the beginning role. A Job Offer letter should include the following:

- Job title
- Start date
- Salary
- Manager's name
- Employee benefits
- Employment relationship
- Others
- State on the Job Letter the performance of job duties and obligations and compliance with company policies.

EMPLOYEE PERSONA DATA FORM

Employee Personal Data forms provide key data on employees that can be used to keep track of who is working for your company, when, and in what position. It can also be used as an emergency contact information form in any event.

JOB DESCRIPTION AND RESPONSIBILITIES

A JOB DESCRIPTION is a statement, which lists **duties** & **responsibilities** required to perform a particular **job** and expresses what a prospective employee must do when he will get the placement.

Before the new employee starts on a new job, he should know the job description and responsibilities of the job he/she has been hired to perform. The new employee should sign a copy stating that he knows what the hiring person is expecting to be done.

The main points of the job description may include key responsibilities, functions, and duties; education and experience requirements; and any other pertinent information (i.e., scheduling requirements, travel, etc).

BACKGROUND CHECK AUTHORIZATION FORM SIGNED

The Federal Trade Commission (FTC) and Consumer Financial Protection Bureau (CFPB) requires **authorization** before running a tenant or employment **background check** on another person. Have the applicant sign and date the authorization form.

A background check will vary based on the reason the screening is needed. Employers are not the only ones who utilize background checks. A landlord, creditor and insurers also routinely look at various aspects of background checks. An employer will often want to check:

* Credit Report
* Driving Record
* Criminal Record
* Employment History

AUTHORIZATION PRIOR TO RUN A BACKGROUND CHECK

Before to running a Background check, you need to provide the proper disclosure and obtain authorization.

The Federal Trade Commission (FTC) and Consumer Financial Protection Bureau (CFPB) requires authorization before running a tenant or employment background check on another person. This must be a stand-alone document, separate from the actual tenant / employment application. An employer, landlord or creditor must let the applicant know the background checks will be used in the decision-making process and provide the applicant with a copy of their Summary of Rights under the FCRA.

The applicant must also be provided a written form (separate from the application) with a space for them to include their personal information, name, address, date of birth and social security number if required for the type of background check you wish to obtain. Make sure to list the type of checks you will be doing and include a statement that the information you obtain from the results will be used in the decision-making process. Have the applicant sign and date the authorization form. https://blog.verifirst.com

It is very important to keep the written authorization form within the applicant's file. This will ensure you have proper documentation showing you have authorization should the need arise later. Do not destroy this document. You may black out sensitive information such as the social security number if needed.

COMPLYING WITH THE LAW

Federal law requires compliance when obtaining background checks. Failure to get the applicants authorization or following the proper disclosures can result in legal consequences including lawsuits against you in both state and federal court. Before running background checks, make sure you are up to date with all applicable laws.

W2 TAX FORM

The IRS states the following:

Every employer engaged in a trade or business who pays remuneration, including non-cash or more for the year (all amounts if any income, social security, or Medicare tax was withheld) for services performed by an employee must file a Form W-2 for each employee (even if the employee is related to the employer) from whom:

- Income, social security, or Medicare tax was withheld.
- Income tax would have been withheld if the employee had claimed no more than one withholding allowance or had not claimed exemption from withholding on Form W-4, Employee's Withholding Allowance Certificate.

In other words, Form W-2 is an Internal Revenue Service tax form used to report wages paid to employees and the taxes withheld from them. Employers must complete a Form W-2 for each employee to whom they pay a salary, wage, or other compensation as part of the employment relationship

FORM I-9 AND SUPPORTING DOCUMENTS

Employees must provide documentation to their employers to show their identity and authorization to work.

Under federal law, employers must verify the identity and employment authorization of each person they hire to perform work in the United States, complete and retain a **Form I-9** (Employment Eligibility Verification).

As part of the **Form I-9** process, new hires must present original identity and work authorization documents to their employer to prove that they are authorized to work in the U.S.

The employer must record the document information, sign the form, and return the document(s) to the employee.

What are **Form I-9** Supporting Documents? To prove work authorization, employees may choose which document(s) he or she wants to present from the List of Acceptable Documents. Certain documents such as a US passport show both identity and employment authorization (List A). www.uscis.gov

A simplified summary about the UCSIS and the Form I9, is detailed on the Yale University site where you can find a wide explanation about the Form I9. They state the following: "The U.S. Department of Homeland Security's employment eligibility process requires that employees must present, to their employer, evidence of identity and employment eligibility within three business days of the date employment begins. If an employee is authorized to work, but is unable to present the required document(s) within three business days, they must present a receipt for the application of the document(s) within three business days and the actual document(s) within ninety (90) days."

LISTS OF ACCEPTABLE DOCUMENTS

You may provide a document from List A which establishes both identity and employment eligibility or you may provide a document from List B (establishing your identity) and a document from List C (establishing your employment eligibility).

LIST A Documents that Establish Both Identity and Employment Eligibility	LIST B Documents that Establish Identity	LIST C Documents that Establish Employment Eligibility
OR		AND
1. U.S. Passport (unexpired or expired)	1. Driver's license or ID card issued by a state or outlying possession of the United States provided it contains a photograph or information such as name, date of birth, gender, height, eye color and address	1. U.S. Social card issued by the Social Security Administration *(other than a card stating it is not valid for employment)*
2. Permanent Resident Card or Alien Registration Receipt Card (Form I-551)	2. ID card issued by federal, state or local government agencies or entities, provided it contains a photograph or information such as name, date of birth, gender, height, eye color and address	2. Certification of Birth Abroad issued by the Department of State *(form FS-545 or Form DS-1350)*
3. An unexpired foreign passport with a temporary I-551 stamp	3. School ID card with a photograph	3. Original or certified copy of a birth certificate issued by a state, county, municipal authority or outlying possession of the United States bearing an official seal
4. An unexpired Employment Authorization Document that contains a photograph (Form I-766, I-688, I-688A, I-688B)	4. Voter's registration card	4. Native American tribal document
	5. U.S. Military card or draft record	5. U.S. Citizen ID Card *(Form I-197)*
5. An unexpired foreign passport with an unexpired Arrival-Departure Record, Form I94, bearing the same name as the passport and containing an endorsement of the alien's nonimmigrant status, if that status authorizes the alien to work for the employer	6. Military dependent's ID card	6. ID Card for use of Resident Citizen in the United States *(Form I-179)*
	7. U.S. Coast Guard Merchant Mariner Card	7. Unexpired employment authorization document issued by DHS *(other than those listed under List A)*
	8. Native American tribal document	
	9. Driver's license issued by a Canadian government authority	
	For persons under age 18 who are unable to present a document listed above:	
	10. School record or report	
	11. Clinic, doctor, or hospital record	
	12. Daycare or nursery school record	

WHAT IS A CONTRACT?

Similar to an offer letter, a contract lays out the details of a role and includes many of the same key pieces of information. However, unlike an offer letter, a contract typically has a specific time period attached to it and is used in cases where employers are hiring someone for a certain amount of time. Contracts are likely to be used in the following cases:

* Freelance positions
* Temp to perm positions
* Contract positions for specific projects

Like offer letters, contracts are time sensitive and generally require a signature within about a week.

ARE YOU LIKELY TO RECEIVE BOTH AN OFFER LETTER AND A CONTRACT?

Generally speaking, the answer is no. Although offer letters and contracts serve similar purposes, they are generally used for different types of work. While an offer letter indicates the beginning of a long-term full-time role, a contract is more often used to an established short-term work relationship or one that does not fit the terms for full-time employment. For example, while you might work standard full-time hours on a contract, you are unlikely to receive the same benefits as a full-time employee such as health insurance or a 401k plan.

PRO TIP: Temp to perm employees (employees who begin as contractors before transitioning to full-time members of the team) are the exception to the rule. Since these types of employees start off as contracted workers, they work on a contract basis before receiving their offer letter to join the team full-time.

Knowing the difference between an offer letter and a contract is a great way to manage your expectations when it comes to accepting a job offer. This will ensure that you know what each type of offer means and that you are able to make an informed decision about accepting it.

-

www.ingramcontent.com/pod-product-compliance
Lightning Source LLC
Chambersburg PA
CBHW030543220526
45463CB00007B/2954